Penelope

Penelope, that vociferous heroine of Thelwell's famous riding academy, has something to say on almost every aspect of the human condition, however hair-raising her own may be at the time. Ponies and philosophy go hand-in-hand when Penelope is around.

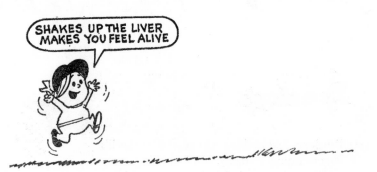

Penelope
by
thelwell

A METHUEN PAPERBACK

First published in 1972
by Eyre Methuen Ltd
11 New Fetter Lane, London EC4P 4EE
Copyright © 1972 by Norman Thelwell
and Beaverbrook Newspapers Ltd
This paperback edition published 1975
by Methuen Children's Books Ltd
Printed in Great Britain by Richard Clay (The Chaucer Press) Ltd
Bungay, Suffolk

ISBN 0 416 55230 7

" I DON'T THINK MUCH OF HIS SEAT.

This book is based on a series which appeared
in the Sunday Express

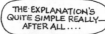

I THINK KIPPER'S SUFFERING FROM SWEET-ITCH, MAGNUS. AS AN AUTHORITY ON EQUINE DISORDERS I'D BE GLAD IF YOU'D TAKE A LOOK AT HIM!

SWEET-ITCH IS A COMMON COMPLAINT WITH CHILDREN'S PONIES, I'M AFRAID. THERE'S FAR TOO MUCH OF IT ABOUT!

OH DEAR! OH DEAR! I'M AFRAID IT'S SWEET-ITCH ALRIGHT!

WHAT DO YOU ADVISE?

GROOM THEM CAREFULLY OUT OF HIS COAT AND DON'T EAT ANY MORE TOFFEES ON HORSEBACK!

" I'LL BE GLAD WHEN SHE GETS INTERESTED IN BOYS. "

LET'S COLLECT OUR THINGS AND GO DOWN TO THE SEA-SIDE, FIONA!
LOVE TO!
SMELL THAT OZONE, PENELOPE! IT'S GREAT TO GET AWAY FROM IT ALL!
HURRY UP FIONA! I CAN'T WAIT!
IT'S THE CHANGE THAT DOES YOU GOOD!

" COME ALONG GIRLS . PLAY TIME'S OVER "

I'VE JUST SEEN A HORRIBLE LITTLE HORSEFLY!

SO HAVE I !

" WHAT A SHAME! THERE GOES HER EGG AND SPOON. "

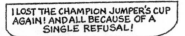

ALL RIGHT!
ALL RIGHT!
HAVE IT
YOUR OWN
WAY

GO IN THE CAR!

" SHE'S NOT MAKING VERY RAPID PROGRESS, I'M AFRAID "

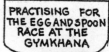

WERE YOU DISAPPOINTED, PENELOPE, WHEN KIPPER ONLY CAME THIRD IN THE SHOW JUMPING?

NO! I THINK HE DID WELL WHEN YOU CONSIDER THAT HE ALWAYS STARTS OFF WITH A HANDICAP OF FOUR FAULTS!

WHICH FOUR FAULTS?

HIS **LEGS**!

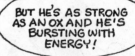

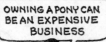

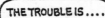

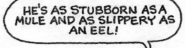

" SHE LOVES THAT PONY — NEVER OUT OF THE SADDLE."

I'M WORRIED ABOUT KIPPER, FIONA. HE'S GOT A TOUCH OF INSOMNIA!

I'M SURE I'M RIGHT BUT I'D APPRECIATE A SECOND OPINION

THERE! DID YOU SEE THAT EYELID FLICKER?

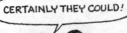

" HURRY UP!   I'M ON HORSEBACK . "

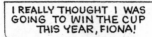

EVERY DAY THE NEWSPAPERS ARE FULL OF SUCH HORRIBLE THINGS, IT MAKES ME WORRY ABOUT WHAT'S GOING TO BECOME OF US ALL!

THERE'S NO SENSE IN WORRYING ABOUT THE FUTURE, FIONA!

YOU'VE GOT TO LEARN HOW TO ENJOY TODAY!

I HATE HAIR-WASHING NIGHT, MAGNUS! IT'S A DREADFUL CHORE!

I HATE IT! DO YOU HEAR? I HATE IT!

HOT WATER! SHAMPOO! ALL THE RINSING DRYING, BRUSHING, COMBING...

THE MESS AND MUDDLE! ALL THAT CLEARING UP! AND THEN NEXT MORNING...

...I CAN'T DO A THING WITH IT!